The Kama Sutra

The Erotic Essence of India

Astrolog publishing house

Editor: Bret Norton
Cover Design: Na'ama Yaffe
Language Consultant: Marion Duman
Layout and Graphics: Daniel Akerman
Production Manager: Dan Gold

P.O. Box 1123, Hod Hasharon 45111, Israel
Tel: 972-9-7412044
Fax: 972-97442714
E-Mail: info@astrolog.co.il
Astrolog Web Site: www.astrolog.co.il

ISBN 965-494-089-2

Printed in Israel
10 9 8 7 6 5 4 3 2 1

contents

A visitor to the ancient temples which are scattered all over India, carved into the mountainside or built of stone, is immediately struck by the sculptures that adorn the temples. These sculptures depict a never-ending tableau of men and women clasped and enmeshed in hundreds of positions, the purpose of which is the attainment of the optimal physical pleasure.

During a period of approximately one thousand years, extending from the fifth century BC to the fifth century AD, splendid temples were constructed in India, and tens of erotic literary masterpieces were written. The Indians (especially those belonging to the upper castes, and the wealthy, who lived lives of luxury) considered reaching heights of physical pleasure both a social and a personal goal.

There are four realms in a person's life: the realm of religion and morality; the material realm; the spiritual realm; and the realm of physical pleasure. A person cannot live a full life without a combination of the four. Love, desire, sexual compatibility, stimulation, and sexual release all uplift the kama, the realm of physical pleasure, and enable the person to achieve a fuller life.

Just as a person is compelled to study and develop the realm of religion and morality, to support his household and himself and increase his assets, to enrich and purify his spirit - so must he be acquainted with and develop every characteristic of his body, as well as every action that can enhance his desire and his enjoyment.

The pleasures of the flesh are a natural and essential part of human life. The Indians believed that the pleasures of the flesh are attained by means of the five senses, which influence the body either directly or by stimulating the imagination. Sexual intercourse must involve the senses of sight, hearing, touch, smell and taste. This is the reason why the erotic masterpieces depict themes such as dancing and music, body odors, male and female bodies, and other topics which are not necessarily connected with the actual sexual act.

However, the greatest pleasure that can be experienced by the human body is that produced by the contact, joining, and friction of the genitals - the male *Lingam* and the female *Yoni*. The closer, longer and more powerful the contact, the greater the physical pleasure. Hence the great importance of the positions described in the erotic works of art of India - positions whose purpose is to cause the contact between Lingam and Yoni to produce maximum pleasure, taking into account the physical and psychological characteristics of the man and the woman.

Over a period of about one thousand years, scores of erotic masterpieces were written in India. Some presented their readers with a detailed sex guide, while others focused on a certain aspect of sex. Several books dealt with classifying and matching men and women, while others concentrated on general topics in the realm of the pleasures of the flesh. We find books for virgins who are on the threshold of initiation, for courtesans or old women; we will find books addressed to handsome men with large Lingams, as well as to men who are disabled or deformed; books which deal with sexual positions and variations alongside books which are devoted solely to the arts of kissing, caressing, and scratching.

These erotic works were far-reaching, and were sometimes decorated with exquisite paintings and drawings (some of which are presented, in all their magnificence, in this book). Only kings, nobles and people of wealth could afford to own a collection of these splendid works of art.

Today, one particular work is well known, and is representative of Indian erotica: the *Kama Sutra*. The *Kama Sutra* is "a guide to the art of desire, its enhancement and fulfillment," or what is nowadays known as "a guide to perfect sex."

No one knows when the *Kama Sutra* appeared in its final form. It seems that sometime between the third and the fifth centuries, the Indian scholar Vatsyayana decided to condense the content of scores of works that had been produced before his time into one book. This book was called the *Kama Sutra*.

In the *Kama Sutra*, the author presents detailed information (derived from both other sources and his personal experience (encompassing all the subjects concerning men and women, as well as the forms of contact between the sexes. Courtship, adornment, marriage, dimensions, customs, kissing, sexual intercourse, stimulation of intercourse, unconventional forms of intercourse, sexual relations between members of the same sex, sexual positions ... no area in the realm of sex is omitted in the *Kama Sutra*. Even today, hundreds of years later, in the Western world (ostensibly so permissive (no erotic work exists that is anywhere near as all-encompassing and in-depth as the *Kama Sutra*.

Although the background of the *Kama Sutra* is fifth-century Indian society, which led a comfortable and hedonistic existence, saturated with eroticism, everyone in the contemporary Western world can benefit from the advice and instructions contained in the book.

This book presents extracts which constitute the essence of the various sections of the Kama Sutra. It is based on the definitive, scientific translation of the book from Sanskrit into English, without altering any of the descriptions or concepts of the original. The full-color pictures which accompany the text come from original Indian editions of the *Kama Sutra*.

The last years have witnessed a revival of the *Kama Sutra* in the West. The information pertaining to human sexuality gathered in India over a period of thousands of years is more comprehensive and profound than any of the sex manuals produced in the West.

It is my hope that the Western reader of this magnificent edition of the *Kama Sutra* will derive great pleasure from the world's most famous erotic masterpiece.

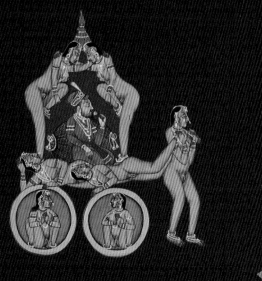

Conversations

What is the most beautiful sight the eye can behold? The face of a woman in love.

What is the perfume whose fragrance is more delightful than any other?

The fragrance of her breath.

What is the loveliest sound the ear can hear?

The voice of the beloved woman.

What is the sweetest taste of all?

The taste of the nectar of her lips.

What is the softest touch of all?

The touch of her body.

What is the most pleasant thing a man can imagine?

The sight of his beloved's beauty.

For when a young woman is in love, everything about her delights the eye and inflames the heart.

The young virgin is like a rosebud about to bloom; the bud grows pure and unblemished in the shade of the leaves, protected from all evil; but when the bud blooms and opens for all to see, the flower will be exposed to every passer-by; and after a thousand passers-by have looked at it, one will seek the purity of the bud in the blooming flower – to no avail.

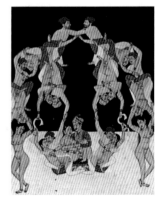

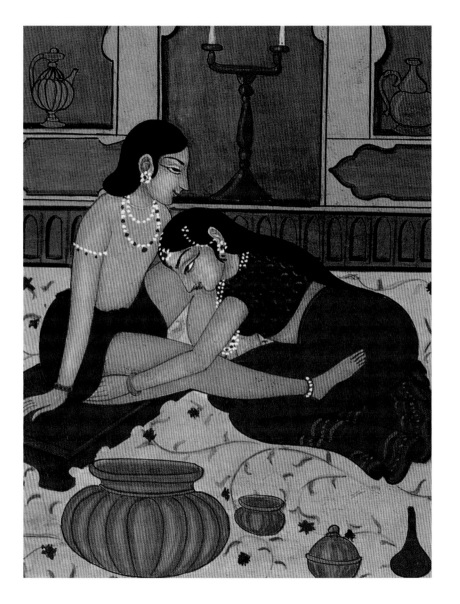

Beautiful women,
with sparkling deer eyes, are
a delight to the eyes of a man:
    When they are far away, we await
their return.
    When they are nearby, we rush into
their arms.
    And once in their arms, we are
unable to tear ourselves away.

There are four types of women, each with its own qualities

Women are divided into four types, according to their physical and moral characteristics. The perfect type is the *Padmini*, or Lotus woman; she embodies all the good qualities, and the list of qualities is long:

She is as beautiful as the lotus blossom; she is *Rati* [pleasure, desire] incarnate.

Her slim waist emphasizes her full thighs, and her gait is proud and dignified, like that of a swan.

Her body is shapely and soft, and she smells like the sandalwood tree; she carries herself like a cypress tree, and holds her head like the top of a pine tree.

Her delicate, smooth skin is as soft to the touch as the trunk of a newborn elephant. Its color is golden when light shines on it.

Her voice resembles the call of the male Kokila bird to its mate; her words are like nectar of the gods to hear. Her perspiration has the scent of musk; every perfume suits her fragrance; bees hover about her as if she were a flower overflowing with pollen.

Her silky hair is long and wavy, black as a panther's fur, a halo around her face – like a full moon in the darkness of the sky – and her tresses flow like waterfalls over her rounded shoulders.

Her forehead is smooth; her eyebrows are perfect crescents, and when she is in the throes of passion, her brows resemble the god Kama's bow.

Her marvelously shaped eyes sparkle, as gentle and soft as a deer's, with a hint of pink in their corners. Her pupils are as black as the night, and contain sparks like stars in the heavens. Her long, silky lashes are a window to her soft glance.

Her nose is like the sesame bud, starting off straight and then curving like a parrot's beak.

Her full pink lips are like a bud about to flower, or as red as sea coral or the bimba fruit.

Her teeth are as white as jasmine from the Arabian desert, and look like ivory. When she smiles, her teeth are like white pearls on a coral bed.

Her slender neck is like an ivory tower placed on the arches of her lovely shoulders. Her arms are as long as the branches of the mango tree, and her hands as delicate as the branches of the ashoka tree.

Her breasts are as full and firm as the fruit of the pear tree – like two inverted gold goblets adorned with rosy buds.

Her shapely back is as supple as a serpent's, and blends in perfect harmony with the twin globes of her broad buttocks and firm thighs, like the proud swell of a pigeon's breast.

Her navel is deep, and its color is that of a ripe raspberry, placed clearly in the center of her round belly. In the skin above her waist are three delicate folds, like a girdle surrounding her body.

Her buttocks are wonderful. She is like Nitambini, the water nymph.

Like the lotus blooming in the shade of the reeds, so her small Yoni, below her groin which is generously adorned with delicate pubic hair, opens mysteriously.

The fragrance of her groin is like that of a lily in bloom. Her round, smooth, firm legs are like the trunk of the banana plant. Her small feet are joined to her legs like lotus flowers to their stems.

When she dips herself in a hidden spring, the sight engenders love. The gods themselves tremble with desire when they see the Padmini in the water.

There are gleaming pearls on her ears, and a pendant of precious stones on her breast. Her beauty is enhanced by jewels – few in number – on her arms and ankles.

She loves white dresses, white flowers, handsome jewels and rich garments. She wears a white dress made of fine white muslin.

She eats little and sleeps lightly, and she likes light, sweet dishes.

She is skilled in all thirty-two ways of playing the radha. As with those who love Krishna, her singing is harmonious, accompanied by the sounds of the veena, which she plucks with slender fingers.

When she dances, her body and arms move in perfect harmony, even though, because of her great modesty, she does everything in her power to conceal the charms of her body.

Her conversation is pleasant and her smile warm; she is amenable and responsive, and enjoys amusements and pleasure.

Her talents enable her to accomplish any task that she is given.

She avoids the company of dishonest people; lies are loathsome to her.

She adores and worships Brahma, her father and her gods; she never tires of listening to the conversation of Brahmans.

She is generous to the poor and gives of her husband's possessions to the oppressed.

She enjoys making love with her husband, and knows how to enhance his desire with her caresses.

The god of love will lose himself in endless pleasures at her side.

She is faithful to her husband and will not share her love with any other man. Her life, her thoughts and her emotions are devoted to her husband.

All her qualities are perfect.

Padmini, a woman of many qualities, was given many names by poets, and each name serves to emphasize her qualities.

Love's treasure! The purest of women! The woman in whom love will overcome desire! The woman of love! The woman to whose love nothing can be compared.

After the Padmini comes the *Chitrini*, or the artful woman.

The Chitrini is quick-thinking and has an easy-going temperament; her neck is firm; her hair

is drawn into braids and falls over her broad shoulders like black snakes; her voice resembles honeycomb; her thighs are narrow, but they share the roundness of the banana plant. She is as faithful as a tame elephant; she enjoys pleasure, and is capable of arousing, varying and receiving it. Her gait is rhythmic, like that of a mare; her large breasts resemble ripe fruit on a slim branch; sparse hair grows in her groin, and beneath it, a soft Yoni opens up to the ones she loves.

When she makes love, her juices flow like a spring; she is well-versed in all the pleasures of love and sexual intercourse.

After the Chitrini comes the *Hastini*, or the Elephant woman.

The Hastini has coarse hair that grows in curls down her head; her sharp glance embarrasses the god of love and makes young girls blush. Her large, solid body is adorned with many jewels, and her dresses are bedecked with flowers. Her large, firm breasts are like two golden vases. She eats great quantities, like the elephant; her perspiration is pungent, and her Yoni is so wide that only curls of hair cover the mound above it. Her lovemaking is energetic and noisy.

After the Hastini comes the *Shankhini* or Pig woman.

Her hair is frizzy and tied back; her face is withered, and her lust for men is engraved on it. Her body resembles that of a pig. The Shankhini is always angry, sulking, and complaining. Her breasts and belly smell of fish. She is not clean, eats anything and everything, and is in the habit of sleeping limitlessly.

Her eyes are repulsive, and her glance dull. Her groin is coarse and hairy, and her Yoni is wide and rough. When she makes love, her juices smell of fish, and she is energetic to the point of endangering her lover.

There are four types of men, as lovers or husbands, in parallel with the four types of women:

The Hare man, active and vital, suits the Padmini woman.

The Deer man, who is searching for perfection in sexual intercourse, suits the Chitrini woman.

The Bull man, who has a bull's strength and temperament, suits the Hastini woman.

The Horse man, whose lust is like a stallion in heat, suits the Shankhini woman.

20

As the poets say:

If you are searching, looking for the Padmini,
Only among ten thousand thousand women will you find her.
If you are searching, looking for the Chitrini,
Only among ten thousand women will you find her.
If you want a Hastini woman,
You will find her among a thousand.
And if you desire a Shankhini,
You will find one like her on every corner.

The sexual preferences of the various women of India

 man, especially one who is embarking on a journey, must learn to know women's love everywhere, so that he knows. how to behave without affronting the customs of the place, or exposing himself to scorn and derision during sexual intercourse.

The women of central India, between the Ganges and Jumna, are restrained in their behavior, and never permit a man to leave tooth marks or nail imprints on them.

The women of Avantika like simple sexual intercourse, and their interest is in the act itself rather than its variations.

The women of Maharashtra enjoy all sixty-four variations of the *Kama Sutra*; they utter obscenities during intercourse, and their sensuality is extraordinary.

The women of Pataliputra enjoy intercourse, and are skilled at it, like the women mentioned above, but they do not utter obscenities, and their behavior in public is modest and virtuous.

The women of Dravida, no matter how much they are kissed and caressed, are slow to be aroused and slow to reach orgasm.

The women of Vanavasi are indifferent to caresses, loathe physical contact, and retort angrily when they receive indecent proposals.

The women of Avanti are eager for sexual intercourse of any kind.

The women of Malwa are keen to be kissed and slapped, but do not like bites and scratches.

The women of Punjab are crazy about Auparishtaka, pleasuring of the Yoni with mouth and tongue.

The women of Aparaitika and Lat are eager for sexual intercourse, and murmur "Sit, sit" softly during the entire act.

The women of Avda have overwhelming urges, and their love juices overflow endlessly, to the extent that they have to take medications to stop the flow.

The women of Avdahra have flexible bodies and are willing to try any position.

The women of Ganda are delicate in body and spirit.

25

The seduction of a young girl, with the intention of marrying her

irst, the suitor must win the trust of the young girl's older sister, or an older female relative. It is incumbent upon him to prove to this woman that he is well-versed in all sixty-four arts of love of the *Kama Sutra* that a man has to know, both in theory and in practice.

He must always wear nice clothes and make a good impression on those who see him; young girls fall in love easily with good-looking, well-dressed suitors.

27

The young girl reveals her inner thoughts of love through special signs: She never looks directly into the man's face, and feels ashamed and embarrassed if he looks at her. She accidentally exposes her arms to him; she watches him for a long time when he departs, lowers her gaze when he turns to her, and answers his questions hesitantly, in brief sentences. She is happy to be among the people with whom he spends a lot of time, and she speaks to her friends in a special tone of voice that he can hear even if he is at a distance from her. She does everything in her power to remain in his company for as long as possible, and their parting is lingering. She can kiss and caress a child sitting on her lap, in this way hinting at her feelings toward the man, and is friendly to all his friends and acquaintances. She must behave politely toward his servants, and she must take advantage of any opportunity that arises to visit his home.

She must ensure that one of her friends shows the man her earrings, necklaces, and the rest of her jewels; she must wear the jewelry that the man has given her whenever she can. Every time someone says something disparaging about the man, or mentions a former suitor of hers, she must scowl angrily.

A man who falls in love with a woman, and sees from the hints she drops that his feelings are reciprocated, must unite his body with hers. A young girl is ensnared games and amusements, a young woman by the man's skill in the arts of the *Kama Sutra*, and a mature woman by a trusted intermediary who makes contact between the two.

When he has conquered the young girl's heart, the suitor must continue the art of seduction:
When he is with her, he must hold her hand, as lovers do, and show her the blossoms and buds, tell her about his dreams – especially those about rendezvous with beautiful women – and whenever they are in the company of others, he should touch her arm, rub his leg against hers,

and particularly press her toes firmly with his big toe.

If she does not object, he should hold her foot in his hand and squeeze it, and caress her toes with his fingers. When he freshens his mouth with water containing fragrant leaves, he sprays the water in an arc from his mouth onto her head.

When he comes upon an isolated spot with her, he should caress her lovingly, reveal his passion – but without harming or angering her.

When he has the opportunity to sit beside her on a bed or under a canopy, he should ask her to go to an isolated spot with him, and there he should reveal his love for her in actions, not in words. He takes her hands and puts them on his forehead.

When she comes to his house, he must keep her there as long as possible. When she leaves the house, he must implore her to come and visit him again soon.

The man must never forget the words of the sages: "A man, however much he may be in love with a woman, will not win her without whispering words of love in her ear."

Finally, when the young girl has succumbed to his charms, he can enjoy her loveliness.

If the man is unable to perform these steps alone, he must request the assistance of the older woman whose trust he gained, and she will entice the young girl to go to the man's house and be with him.

"If the time and place are suitable, no woman will oppose the wishes of the man she loves."

Different kinds of sexual intercourse

here are seven different kinds of sexual intercourse:

Spontaneous intercourse: A couple of lovers love each other and make love as a result of mutual attraction.

The game of love, when the woman comes from a family of high standing, is quite enchanting. First the woman cries, "No! No!" and remains indifferent to her lover's caresses. Then her desires ignite, but there is still a measure of modesty in her behavior; her opposition weakens and her aggressiveness disappears; finally, passion overwhelms her, and when she discards all her inhibitions, she receives the blessing of the desire burning in her body.

Sexual intercourse following prolonged desire: The man and the woman have loved each other for a long time, but it was difficult for them to meet; or one of the couple returned from a journey; or the couple made up after a quarrel.

In this case, both members of the couple are burning with desire and are in a hurry to make love and reach mutual satisfaction.

Sexual intercourse in marriage: This occurs between a married couple whose love is still dormant, like a seed buried in the earth before the rains.

Sexual intercourse of forced love: The man performs the act of love after arousing himself through his knowledge of the *Kama Sutra* – kisses, caresses, and embraces; or copulation when each of the couple loves someone else.

In these cases, they must use all the secrets of the *Kama Sutra* to arouse and preserve their desire.

Sexual intercourse of the other love: One of the couple, during intercourse, imagines that he is in the arms of the object of his real love.

Sexual intercourse for release: The woman is the servant or the water bearer, and her status is lower than that of the man, so that the sexual act is meant only for the man's release. In this case, the act is direct and quick, with no foreplay or gratitude afterwards.

Sexual intercourse of lust: This occurs between a noblewoman and a peasant, or an educated man and a peasant's daughter; the deed is brief and crude, unless the woman is unusually beautiful.

Potions that increase virility during sexual intercourse

tir a little white pepper into sweet milk and add: a little auchala root or Sanseviera or roxburghina seeds; essence of the badisram plant; juice of the kyuti and the shirica; a mixture of asparagus stalks, honey and the common mistletoe plant; the Premna spinosa fruit; sweet milk in which a billy-goat's genitals have been cooked; a mixture of honey, sugar and ghee, in equal proportions; each of these potions will increase the man's virility limitlessly.

Crushed sparrow's eggs, together with sweet milk, will enable the man to satisfy many women.

Mixtures of white pepper and honey; or the flesh of a bird of prey and honey; or the vagjranee and chalk powder; or crushed mango pit and the bark of the sioss tree – these mixtures smeared on the Lingam will turn it into a tree trunk whose tip will not bend toward the earth.

Potions must not be used for inspiring love or increasing virility for sexual intercourse in a way that may be harmful to health, or if the potion demands the killing of an animal, or an ugly deed.

Potions that are good for men are those that are not harmful to their health, nor do they contradict religion or tradition.

Positions that increase desire

hen a man and a woman perform sexual intercourse standing up, leaning against each other or against a wall or a column, it is called *supported congress.*

When the man leans against the wall, holds the woman in this arms and hands, while she puts her arms around his neck, lifts her thighs to the middle of his body and moves her body by placing her feet against the wall behind the man, it is called *suspended congress.*

It is recommended that lovers imitate the ways of animals: the dog, the billy-goat, the deer; the mounting and the fierce penetration of the donkey and the cat, the pouncing of the tiger, the pressing of the bear and the galloping of the stallion on the mare; it is good for the man because he will treat the woman like the male animal treats the female.

When a man performs the sexual act with two women simultaneously, it is called *united congress*. This can be done when the two women are lying side by side in the bed, or one is on top of the other, back to stomach, or one is on top of the other stomach to stomach. In all cases, the Yonis must be at the edge of the bed, with the women's feet on the ground. The Lingam goes from Yoni to Yoni, slowly at first, then at a faster speed.

Intercourse with a number of women is called *congress of a herd of cows*; some call this act *an elephant in water*, because the male elephant mates several females while they are bathing in the lake. Another name is *congress of goats*.

When several young men enjoy the body of a woman (possibly the wife of one of them) one after the other or simultaneously, the woman is placed on the body of one of the men, another skewers her Yoni with his Lingam, a third makes use of her mouth, and a fourth holds the middle of her body. They enjoy her body for a long time, exchanging places with one another.

Sometimes, a number of men hire a courtesan to satisfy their desires.

When several women enjoy the body of a man – mainly women of the harem when a man enters the harem by chance – the women make use of his Lingam and body simultaneously or one after the other.

Lower congress is the use of the anus instead of the Yoni.

"A sensual man indulges in all forms of intercourse, and imitates the different birds and animals, since variety – suited to individual preferences and to the customs of the country – inspires passion, love and respect for him in women's hearts."

About the different positions necessary for sexual intercourse

 n high congress, the woman has to be in a position in which her Yoni is wide open. In equal congress, she lies on her back, in the natural position, and allows the man to embrace her in his arms.

In low congress, she must position herself in such away that her Yoni is contracted: sometimes she also has to drink a potion in order to increase her desire and become aroused.

For a reclining Deer woman, there are three positions:

The widely opened position: Her head is lower than her lower abdomen and her buttocks are lifted. The man must massage the Yoni or the Lingam with a lubricant in order to facilitate penetration.

The yawning position: The woman raises and spreads her legs.

The position of the wives of Indra: This position is suitable for sublime superior sexual intercourse, between a horse and a deer. The woman bends her calves on to her thighs and opens them wide. This position requires flexibility and a lot of practice.

The following positions are variations for more simple intercourse:

The clamp: The man lies on the woman with his legs straight and against her legs. This position is good for when the woman is lying on her back, or when the man is lying on his left side with the woman opposite him.

The press: The woman lays her one leg across her lover's thigh and presses his body to hers.

The grip of the mare in heat: The woman squeezes the Lingham with her Yoni using a twisting movement. This position requires a lot of study and practice.

A variety of other positions can be added to the basic ones:

The rising position: The woman lies on her back and lifts both her legs straight up.

The yawning position: The woman raises her legs, opens them and rests them on the man's shoulder.

44

The pressed position: The woman raises and crosses her legs, and the man holds them and presses them with his body on to her breasts; sometimes the women lifts one leg and places it on the man's shoulder, and stretches her other leg out to the side. The man presses her leg on to her breasts, and then the woman switches legs, and so on. This position is called *the splitting of a bamboo*.

The fixing of a nail: One of the woman's legs is straight up, resting on the man's head, and the second is stretched out to the side.

45

The crab position: The woman lifts her legs and bends them toward her stomach.

The packed position: The woman lifts her legs, crosses her thighs and pulls them toward her stomach.

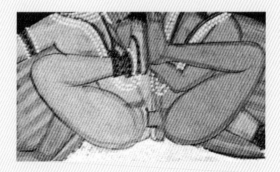

The open lotus: The woman crosses her ankles, leaving her thighs spread wide open. This position, which resembles the position of the wives of Indra, requires a lot of practice.

The turning position: During intercourse, without removing his Lingam from the woman's Yoni, or interrupting the rhythm of their lovemaking, the man turns himself around the woman. This position requires a lot of practice and coordination.

Some people recommend performing sexual intercourse in all possible positions in the bath or in a pool. Others, however, disagree, claiming that intercourse in water is an affront to religious traditions.

When the woman gets down on all fours, like a cow, and her lover mounts her like a bull, it is called *the congress of a cow*. In this position, all the things that are normally done frontally are done with the woman's back toward the man. The man can also stroke the woman's breasts with his right hand, while his left caresses her clitoris, and his Lingam moves in her Yoni. This increases her passion and accelerates her orgasm, so that her climax coincides with the man's.

This is the most favorable position for impregnating a woman, as her uterus is lower than her vulva. It is also a natural position in which the Lingam does not come into contact with the clitoris, instead the man caresses the clitoris with his hand.

47

Classification of men and women according to the size of their genitals

 en can be classified into three types, according to the size of their Lingam: hare, bull, horse. Women can be classified into three types, according to the size of their Yoni: deer, mare, elephant. There are, therefore, three possible equal unions for couples whose genitals are of matching size, and six possible unequal unions for those whose genitals are not of matching size.

Sexual intercourse between a bull and a deer, or between a horse and a mare is considered a high union.

Sexual intercourse between a horse and a deer, in the right way, is considered the highest union.

Sexual intercourse between a hare and a mare, or between a bull and an elephant, is considered a low union

The more enjoyable the sexual act, the more successful it is.

Men and women may also be classified according to the intensity of their sexual climax: weak, medium, and high. The above principles for mating apply here too.

Another classification is according to the time it takes for a man and a woman to reach their climax. The above principles also apply here.

If we were to use all three groups of classifications to match mates, we would reach a large number of possibilities.

The role of the man – especially of the husband – is to employ every available means to ensure that the sexual act is as enjoyable as possible.

During the first act of intercourse between a man and a woman, the man reaches orgasm very quickly, while later it takes him longer. The opposite is true for the woman – at the beginning she is slow, and later she reaches orgasm more quickly.

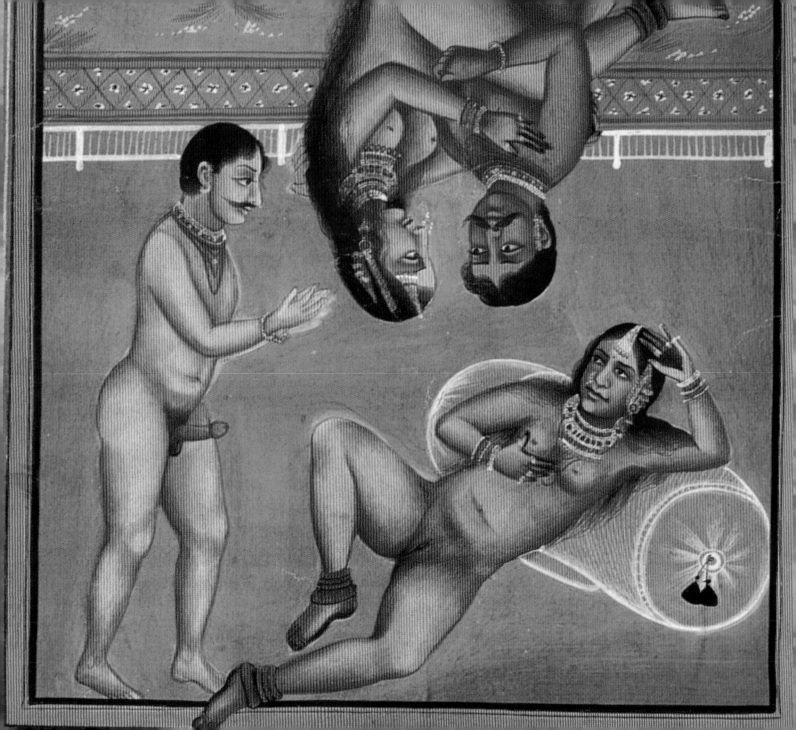

Cases in which love is prohibited

 any people claim that any woman who has already had five lovers can be enjoyed, except for well-known Brahman wives and queens.

Sexual intercourse should not be performed with the following women:

Lepers, lunatics, outcastes, gossips, women who demand sexual satisfaction in public, albinos, or dark-skinned women who smell like corpses.

Female friends, family members, and those who are forbidden for religious reasons.

Those with whom the man played in the sand during childhood, or those to whom the man is obliged or indebted.

Women whose tastes and character are identical to those of the man.

Women who were the man's schoolmates.

The daughters of the nurse or servant, who grew up with the man, or daughters of the family to which the man's family is related by marriage.

The man's female friends must be honest, consistent, faithful and discreet, and have no bad habits.

The various intermediaries used for sexual intrigues

t is permissible for a man to make the acquaintance of people of lower social status who can be of assistance in attaining his heart's and body's desire: washermen, barbers, cowherds, flower sellers, druggists, innkeepers, betel nut sellers, teachers and jesters.

He can also befriend the wives of these men.

Intermediaries, who are required for sexual intrigues, must have the following qualities: skill, obstinacy, access to places, boldness, a sharp eye, and a good memory for reporting everything that is said, done or hinted at.

Good manners, the ability to choose the appropriate time and place, quick decision-making abilities, the ability to deal with the unexpected – these qualities are useful in the intermediary.

There are several kinds of intermediaries or messengers for sexual intrigues:

The intermediary who does everything: This is the one who, the moment he notices a bond of love between two people, will do everything to unite them.

56

The intermediary who acts on her own behalf: This is a messenger who is looking for a man for herself, or, while weaving a sexual intrigue for another woman, will act on her own behalf as well.

The intermediary who acts on her husband's behalf: This is a married woman who assists in her husband's sexual intrigue.

The intermediary who delivers a letter: This is the messenger who delivers a letter, and returns with an oral reply.

The flower deliverer: This is the intermediary who delivers letters hidden in bunches of flowers.

The phantom intermediary: This is the messenger who delivers a message with a double meaning, and announces it in public; its true meaning is understood only by the specific person to whom it is addressed.

Fortune tellers, beggars, servants or maids are intermediaries who quickly gain the trust of the woman.

The intermediary knows how to keep a secret and is adept at describing the woman's charms.

The intermediary does not blush, nor is she embarrassed when she describes in detail the man's love, his wealth, and his expertise in sexual intercourse; in addition, she will tell the woman about the many beautiful women who desire him.

She is also able to effect a reconciliation between lovers after a quarrel.

The role of the man during sexual intercourse

he man must do everything in his power to give the woman pleasure.

If the woman is lying on his bed listening to what he has to say, he must open the belt of her dress; if she objects, he must stifle her objections with kisses.

The best way to begin successful intercourse is by gently sucking the woman's nipples.

When his Lingam is erect, the man must gently touch and caress the woman's body all over.

If the woman is shy, and this is their first meeting, he must place his hand between her thighs and let her close them on his hand.

If the man is with a young girl, he must place his hands on her breasts, cover his hands with hers, and then touch her armpits and neck.

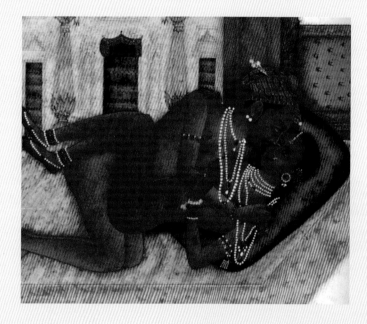

If the man is with a mature woman, he must do everyhing that will satisfy both of their passion – as long as his actions are appropriate to the particular circumstances.

The man must hold her hair and chin in his fingers at all times, and kiss her.

If the woman is very young, she blushes and closes her eyes.

According to the manner in which she reacts to his caresses, the man can know what her preferences are in love games.

"Regardless of what the man is doing for his own pleasure, he must always make sure that he presses to his body the part of the woman's body which she is looking at."

When the woman is pleasured and climaxes, she shows this in several ways:

Her body is relaxed, her eyes closed, she has shed her inhibitions, and she constantly tries to bring the Yoni and the Lingam as tightly together as possible.

When the woman does not experience pleasure, she pounds the bed with her fists and prevents the man from moving away; she is tense, and bites and kicks and continues to make sexual movements even after the man has finished.

In such cases, the man must rub the Yoni with his hand and fingers (like the elephant does with its trunk) before penetration, until the Yoni is wet; only then should the Lingam penetrate the Yoni.

If the woman has not reached orgasm by the time the man finishes, he continues to rub her Yoni with his hand until she climaxes.

There are nine things that the man must do during intercourse:

Penetration or *moving the organs forward:* The Lingam penetrates the Yoni directly.

Rotation: The man holds his Lingam in his hand and turns it around the opening of the Yoni.

Hammering: The Lingam strikes the upper part of the Yoni, like a hammer striking a nail.

Drilling: The Lingam strikes and presses the lower part of the Yoni.

Pressing: The Lingam is inside the Yoni, pressing it for a long time without moving.

Thrusting: The Lingam is withdrawn to some distance from the Yoni, and then penetrates it deeply with one thrust; a series of these blows fills the Lingam with passion, and the faster the rhythm, the greater the woman's pleasure.

Thrust of the boar: The Lingam rubs one side of the Yoni each time it penetrates.

Thrust of the bull: The Lingam rubs both sides of the Yoni each time it penetrates

Fluttering of the sparrow: The Lingam remains inside the Yoni, and moves up and down in short, rapid movements; this generally takes place toward the end of the sexual act, when the man feels that he on the verge of orgasm.

What happens when the woman takes the initiative

 nder certain circumstances, especially when the man is tired after trying to reach orgasm for a long time (and there are men whose Lingam remains erect indefinitely if they do not ejaculate), the woman can take the initiative. Sometimes, when she does this, she is attracted by the variation and novelty in the situation.

There are two possibilities: When the woman, during intercourse, climbs onto the man's body without interrupting the sexual rhythm; or when the woman assumes the role of the man from the beginning of the act.

In the second case, she approaches the man with her hair loose and decorated with flowers, smiling warmly, and presses her breasts onto his chest, kissing his body softly – just as he does when he wants to excite her – saying: "You conquered my heart and body – and now I am going to conquer you until you beg for mercy!"

And from this point, with a mixture of shyness and passion, hesitation and confidence, she will bring their sexual union to a pleasurable conclusion.

Besides the nine things a man must do during intercourse, there are three additional ones that the woman can do:

The tongs: She holds the Lingam inside her Yoni, pulling it inward with sucking movements, and presses firmly, remaining like this for as long as possible.

The spinning top: During intercourse, the woman raises her legs and turns around with the Lingam inside her, like a wheel revolving on its axle.

The swing: The woman rotates the lower part of her body while the Lingam is at the opening of her Yoni. This action is reminiscent of the rotation performed by the man while holding his Lingam in his hand.

When the woman is tired, she rests her head on her lover's shoulder and remains in that position, without separating her Yoni from his Lingam. After she has rested, the man turns her onto her back and resumes their lovemaking.

The young woman who conquers a man

 young woman, who, in spite of being blessed with great beauty, fine qualities, and a good upbringing, is a member of a low-caste family, and therefore does not have any suitable suitors, or a young woman who is an orphan, with no relatives to help her – must find a suitable husband for themselves.

She has to try and capture the heart of a young, good-looking, highly sexed man, or a man whose nature will allow him to marry a woman even without his parents' consent.

She must use every stratagy possible to ensnare him, meeting him and speaking to him often. Her mother and other female relatives must help by arranging frequent meetings in other houses between her and the intended husband. The young woman must try to remain alone with the man, in safe places where they will not be disturbed, and every now and then she must bring him a gift of flowers, perfumes, or betel nuts and leaves.

She must show him her expertise at massage – while scratching him with her nails. She must discuss subjects of interest to him, and especially direct the conversation to the various ways in which a young man can win the heart of a young woman.

Even in the case where the young woman loves the man, she may not make the first move – she must encourage the man to approach her, and receive the signals of his love as if she does not notice his passion for her.

When he tries to kiss her, she must decline at first. When he wants to indulge in sexual intercourse, she must refuse. When he tries to touch her intimate places, she must make it difficult for him to do so, allowing him only a light, superficial contact.

Only when the girl is sure of the man's love for her, and he has promised to marry her in the proper fashion, may she surrender to him.

After she has lost her virginity in this way, she can tell all her friends.

It can be said about kisses:
What you like,
do to your lover,
What you gained from him, he
willgain from you.
A kiss for a kiss,
An embrace for an embrace,
A caress for a caress.

About the kisses that precede and accompany the act of love

uring their first meetings, lovers are advised not to indulge in too much kissing, caressing and other actions that precede actual intercourse; but these things can be done for enjoyment and within measure.

A woman can be kissed on her forehead, eyes, cheeks, neck, chest, breasts, lips, and inside her mouth.

It is recommended that a woman be kissed at the place where her thighs join, along the length of her arms, and on her navel.

A young woman may be given three kinds of kisses: the superficial kiss, the sucking kiss, and the licking kiss.

The superficial kiss is the simplest, when the lovers' lips just touch.

The sucking kiss occurs when the young girl takes the man's lower lip between her lips and pulls it toward her mouth with a sucking movement.

The licking kiss occurs when the young girl brushes her lover's lips with her tongue, and, closing her eyes, places her hands in his.

Some, however, divide the kinds of kisses into four:

The straight kiss: The man's lips are pressed directly onto his beloved's lips, face to face.

The inclined kiss: The lovers incline their heads toward each other and offer their lips to each other.

The turned kiss: One of the lovers turns the other one's face by holding the hair and chin, and then kisses them.

The pressed kiss: This occurs when one of the lovers catches the other's lower lip between his lips and presses hard. The lower lip can also be held between two fingers, touched with the tongue, and then pressed hard with the upper lip, which enhances desire – and this is known as *the greatly pressed kiss.*

The lovers sit opposite each other, waiting to see who will manage to catch the other one's lip in a pressed kiss. If the woman loses, she has to protest loudly, wave her hands in the air, and demand another go. If she loses again, she should emphasize her disappointment: she must take advantage of a moment when the man is distracted, or wait until he falls asleep, and then catch his lower lip between her teeth and grasp it tightly, without allowing him to get away. Then she bursts out laughing, cries out loud, and teases her lover. She skips and dances in front of him, says meaningless things to him, flutters her eyelashes and winks at him.

More experienced lovers refine and expand the kissing game.

When the man kisses the woman's upper lip, and she in turn kisses his lower lip, this is *the kiss of the upper lip*.

When one of the lovers sucks on both the other's lips, it is called *the clasping kiss*.

When, during the kiss, the lovers' tongues flutter over each other's teeth and into each other's mouths, it is called *the battle of the tongues*.

The kisses can be gentle, demanding, soft or hard, according to the part of the body at which they are directed.

Some people broaden the range of kisses by including the sucking of the nipples – which is a conventional form of lovers' foreplay.

When a woman kisses her lover's face while he is sleeping, it is called *a kiss that kindles love*.

When a woman kisses her lover while he is distracted or otherwise engaged, it is called *a kiss that turns away*.

When a man returns home late at night, finds his beloved asleep in bed, and kisses her in her sleep in order to indicate his desire for intercourse, it is called *a kiss that awakens*. Women who are experienced in the ways of love pretend to be fast asleep when their man comes home in order to be kissed in this way.

When someone kisses the reflection (in a mirror or in a pool of water) of their beloved, it is called *the kiss showing intention*."

When someone kisses the child sitting on his lap, or a picture or a statue, while his beloved is watching him, this is t*he third-party kiss*.

At night, in a hall where people are watching a performance, or are gathered for a meeting, if a man approaches a woman and kisses her fingers, if she is standing, or her toes, if she is seated; or if a woman, while massaging her lover's body, places her face on his thighs so as to ignite his passion, and kisses his thigh and his big toe – it is known as *the kiss requesting intercourse*.

About embraces

mbraces where lovers demonstrate their love for each other are divided into four kinds: touching, piercing, rubbing, and pressing.

Touching: This occurs when a man "accidentally" manages to touch the side or front of a woman, creating a light contact between his body and hers.

Brushing: This occurs when a woman bends over a seated man, or bends down to pick something up, and in so doing presses her breasts against his body. He can grab hold of her body and even squeeze her breasts.

Rubbing: This occurs when a couple is walking in the dark, or in an isolated place, and the man's body rubs against the woman's.

Pressing: This occurs in similar circumstances when one of the lovers presses the other against a wall or a pillar, presses up close to him/her, and rubs his/her body.

When lovers meet, they can include different parts of their bodies in their embrace. Face to face, chest to chest, Jagdana to Jagdana [sexual organs], thigh to thigh, and even body to body, when the woman, as a sign of her love, lets her hair fall loosely over her shoulders and back.

The *Kama Shastra* mentions four kinds of embraces: the twining of a creeper and the climbing of a tree, in which the man is standing, and the mixture of sesame seed with rice and the dilution of milk and water – embraces which are actually part of the sexual act itself.

In *the twining of a creeper* embrace, the woman wraps herself around the man like a creeper around a tree; she brings her mouth to his for a kiss, all the while chanting quietly, "Sut! Sut!" She smiles at him and looks at him with eyes full of love.

In *the climbing of a tree* embrace, the woman – all the while humming softly – places one of her feet on her lover's foot, and wraps her other leg around his thigh, while she puts one arm behind his back and the other on his shoulders, desiring to climb up to his mouth and suck kisses from him.

In *the mixture of sesame seed with rice* embrace, the lovers are lying down, embracing in such a way that their arms and legs are intertwined like the roots of a tree, and their bodies rub against each other.

In *the dilution of milk and water* embrace, the man and the woman clutch each other with fierce passion, frantic to unite; they do not fear hurt or pain. Their desire is so great that they just want to get into each other's body and become one body and one flesh. The woman can be sitting on the man's knees, lying on her side or lying opposite him on the bed.

As the poets say:

*I*t is good for lovers to learn and know the art of the embrace, because this art has the power to arouse passion; but during the act of love, the lover is occupied with every embrace and every action that increases his desire, even if it is not one of the embraces enumerated in the *Kama Shastra*.

The embraces of the *Shastra* are good for a couple when there is hostility between them; but when the wheel of love is turning on its axle, the actions of the couple are guided by passion.

83

About biting

 iting is permissible wherever kissing takes place, except for the lower lip, inside the mouth, and the eye. Teeth that are good for biting are straight, proportionate to the mouth, shiny, and sharp. Coarse or flawed teeth detract from the pleasure of the bite.

There are different kinds of bites:

The hinted bite: This is done gently and leaves only a red mark which disappears by the next day.

The pulling bite: This bite involves catching the skin between the teeth and pulling it hard.

The piercing bite: This bite involves catching a small piece of skin between the teeth and biting to the point of pain.

The coral and the oyster bite: This is done by biting simultaneously with the teeth and the lips.

The string of pearls bite: This is done by biting with all the teeth and leaving tooth marks in the flesh.

The broken cloud bite: This bite leaves an uneven imprint in the flesh (usually the breasts) due to uneven or gapped teeth

The bite of the boar: This is a hard bite (or series of bites) on the shoulders and breasts which leaves two rows of tooth marks with a red spot between them that does not disappear immediately. It is a sign of intense passion.

The first three bites are made around the lips, the neck, the hollow of the neck and the groin.

The coral and the oyster bite is made on the forehead or the thigh.

Bites that leave marks for a long time are made on the left cheek, where teeth and nail marks are a lovely adornment for every woman.

Nail or teeth marks on an object that belongs to the beloved – jewelry, bunches of flowers or betel leaves – are a sign of the man's passion for his beloved woman.

"When a man bites a woman hard, she must, in her rage, bite him back twice as hard..."

If the woman is aroused, she must grab the man's hair, pull him to her and bite him all over his body, with her eyes closed and while bending over his body.

In public, in the light of day, when the man smiles at his beloved and shows her the teeth marks that she made in his flesh, she must smile shyly and show him the teeth marks that he made in hers.

When a couple acts like this, the flames of their passion will not be quenched for many years.

About the use of fingernails, scratches and nail marks

enerally speaking, nail marks should be imprinted below the armpit, on the neck, the breasts, around the lips, on the Jagdana and the thighs. These marks, exactly like bite marks, are a testimony to burning love between lovers. They should be imprinted during the first meeting, before embarking on a journey, on being reunited after a journey, upon reconciliation, or when the woman, for some reason, is extraordinarily aroused.

Eight nail marks can be imprinted into the flesh: sounding, half-moon, a circle, a line, a tiger's print, a peacock's foot, the leap of a hare, and the petal of a blue lotus.

Sounding is made by a gentle pressure of the nail on the chin, the breasts, the upper lip or the Jagdana, pressure which does not leave a scratch; the body hair is simply flattened and straightens up again, and the sound of the friction of the nail on the hair can be heard. A lover can perform sounding on his beloved while he is massaging her body, and wants her to pay attention to him.

The half-moon is an isolated nail mark on the woman's neck or breasts.

The circle consists of two half-moons imprinted opposite each other, and it is imprinted on the navel, in the delicate folds under the woman's buttocks, and around her groin.

The line is a short scratch which is imprinted anywhere on the body.

The tiger's print is an arc which is imprinted on the breasts and chest.

The peacock's foot is a mark which is imprinted by five fingers on the breasts and the chest. This scratch requires a great deal of skill.

The leap of a hare is a mark which is made with five fingernails around the nipples.

The petal of a blue lotus consists of scratches whose shape is reminiscent of the lotus petal, on the breasts or thighs.

There are many more scratch marks, and in fact, the shapes of scratches are countless. "Everyone knows about the art of scratching and the imprinting of love marks. Variety is a necessity and a fuel for the flames of love..."

90

Courtesans, who are well-versed in all the forms of scratching and finger imprinting, are the most expensive.

Nail marks are not to be made on the bodies of married women, except in very private places, as a refreshing reminder of an act of love and in order to fan the flames of passion. Even when the nail marks and the scratches are old, the sight of them reminds the woman of moments of passion which are liable to be forgotten over the course of time.

A young woman on whose breasts and chest these marks appear, will attract even a strange man like flies to a honeypot.

A man who has scratch and bite marks on his body is loved by women, even those who are not particularly interested in physical love.

About the kinds of slaps and sounds
that accompany the act of love

laps are part of love play. Sexual intercourse can be compared to an argument because of its thousands of varieties, and the ease with which lovers can be swept into a quarrel.

The parts of the body which may be slapped in passion are: the shoulders, the head, the space between the breasts, the back, the Jagdana, the calves, and the sides of the body.

These slaps are administered with the back of the hand, with closed, straight fingers, with the open palm, or with the fist.

When the woman's body receives slaps, she emits eight different kinds of sounds: Para, Phat, Sut, Plat, the sound of thunder, coughing, weeping, and Hin. Sometimes she will make the sound Phut, like something falling into water, and will call out words like: "Mommy! Mommy!" Sometimes she cries out words as if to protect herself, as if to break away from the man, as if she is in pain, or as if she is agreeable to the slaps.

93

Many women imitate insect or bird sounds: buzzing bees, cooing doves, the cuckoo's call, chattering parrots, hissing geese, or shrieking peacocks.

A woman who is sitting on a man's knees may be given a hard blow. She must react with feigned fury and emit sounds of protest and pain.

During intercourse, it is accepted practice to hit the space between the breasts with the back of the hand, matching the accelerating rhythm of the lovemaking, until orgasm is achieved. At that moment, the woman should utter the sound "Hin," or any other sound that the lovers prefer.

When the man whips the woman's head with his fingertips, he emits the sound "Phat," and she must answer with coughing, "Phat" and "Phut."

When the lovers resume kissing and love games, the woman hums and chirps like a bird.

When their passion flares up, and the woman is not accustomed to receiving slaps, she must cry out incessantly, "Stop! Stop!", "Enough already!", "Mommy! Mommy!", "Daddy!" – together with wails and groans, weeping and sounds of thunder.

Towards the end of the sexual act, the man must press his hands hard on the woman's breasts, on her Jagdana or on the sides of her body, and she must answer with a whispering or whistling sound, like a bird.

Auparishtaka, or oral sex

here are two types of male prostitutes: those that dress like men and those that want to be thought of as women. Everything that is done in a woman's Yoni is done in the male prostitute's mouth.

Auparishtaka is the way male prostitutes earn their living. Their clients are men, and the experienced ones are well-versed in the eight kinds of Auparishtaka.

Besides the male prostitutes, there are manservants that perform Auparishtaka on their masters, and there are also men who do it in secret.

Women in the harem who have peculiar tendencies, are in the habit of performing Auparishtaka through oral contact with the Yoni.

There are men who are in the habit of kissing the Yoni as if it were the mouth. In these cases, the man holds the woman's legs, with her head on his thighs, and applies his mouth and tongue to the Yoni before him.

Apadravya, or artificial means of increasing desire

In order to arouse a woman, the man can use what are called Apadravyas, objects which are placed on or around the Lingam to lengthen or thicken it, thus making it suit the size of the Yoni.

These objects are made of gold, silver, copper, iron, bull's horn, various kinds of wood, and leather. They must be well-polished and suited to their purpose in every way. Every man must match the Apadravya to his erect Lingam.

The different types are:

Valaya: It is as long as the Lingam and is placed on it; its surface is uneven and covered with round protrusions.

There is the double Valaya – one on top of the other – and

there are Chudakas, which are rings placed consecutively on the Lingam to create a Valaya which is as long as the Lingam.

The Bracelet is a metal wire which is coiled very tightly around the Lingam, up to the tip.

The Jalaka is a metal tube which is open at both ends, and rough on the outside. The Jalaka must fit the Yoni exactly, and is attached by a belt to the man's waist. Some people use wooden tubes, while others place the Jalaka on the Lingam without a belt. In any event, the Jalaka must be lubricated with oil before use.

100

Some people pierce the skin of the Lingam, as is done with the earlobe, and insert objects which increase the woman's passion into the hole – something like an earring.

There are people who regularly rub substances into the Lingam in order to increase its size and strength; for a month they rub in the webs of a certain insect, and then for two months they rub in oil, and so on. When the Lingam has swollen to huge proportions, the man lies face down on a hammock with a hole in it and lets the Lingam hang down for all to see. In order to combat the pain involved in the swelling of the Lingam, he must apply painkilling and soothing ointments.

A lovers' tryst

he meeting place must be chosen with care – on the shores of a freshwater lake, in a city square, or in another place where people meet in order to become acquainted.

The place where the tryst is to take place must be suitably prepared: the room where they will make love must be at the back of the house, the entrance hall at the front, and everything must be furnished comfortably and tastefully.

Every day, the man must bathe and rub his body with oil; every three days he must apply milk to his body; every four days he must shave his face, and every five or ten days he must shave his body hair.

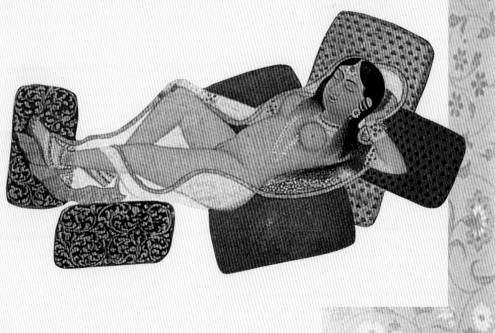

Three meals must be eaten every day – morning, noon and night; one must bathe and rest in the afternoon, wear white clothes, inhale the fragrance of flowers; amuse oneself with relatives in the morning, and enjoy oneself with friends in the afternoon.

After breakfast, it is good to give the parrot a lesson in speaking, or to watch poultry or doves from up close.

In the evening, it is good to sing; the master of the house, sitting comfortably and contentedly with friends, awaits the arrival of his beloved. When she arrives, he welcomes her with love and respect, and she pleasantly greets those present in the room.

When the woman comes to spend the night in her lover's house, she must be freshly bathed, perfumed and suitably dressed. Her lover offers her light refreshments, invites her to sit down on his left, strokes her hair, smoothes her dress, and gently encircles her waist with his right arm; small talk follows, accompanied by jokes, stories and innuendos with an erotic flavor. Then everyone sings together, plays musical instruments, and sips drinks.

When the woman discovers that, as a result of all the above, she is aroused, the master of the house sends his guests off with gifts of flowers, baskets of fruit, and betel leaves.

Now the two lovers are alone. After they have satisfied their desire, they get up very slowly, without looking at each other, and adjourn to the washrooms.

They return to sit together and chew betel leaves. Then the man rubs the woman's body with bark of the sandalwood tree, wraps his left arm around her, whispers sweet nothings into her ear, and lets her sip from the cup he is holding. Together they eat cakes and sweet things, sip clear soup or coconut milk, mango juice or lemon juice. Finally, without being disturbed by anyone, they return to the sweetest fruit of all and savor its delights.

The lovers often go out onto the balcony, where they look at the moon while making love. When the woman is on her knees, her face toward the moon, her lover points out the stars and mentions the names of the zodiacs

The honeymoon

On the tenth night after the conclusion of the wedding ceremonies – and not before – the husband is permitted to be alone with his bride. He speaks to her softly, brings her close to his body, and hugs her to his breast for short periods of time in a way that she finds pleasant. Only after he has embraced her in this manner may he begin to touch her body, first above the waist, since that touch is lighter and simpler.

If the young bride is shy, inexperienced, and the groom does not yet know her very well, he will begin by caressing her in the darkness of night. When he takes a bambola [betel nut or leaves crushed into a ball], he convinces her, even by getting down on his knees, to put the bambola into her mouth. A woman, no matter how irritated or angry she is, will never refuse the man kneeling before her.

109

When he gives her the bambola, he has to kiss her gently on the mouth, and afterwards he speaks to her, asks her questions, and awaits her replies. If her silence persists for a long time, he repeats his questions, since young women, even if they say nothing, listen attentively to every word the man says.

By repeating the question again and again, he will find out if she loves and desires him; and the girl, with her persistent silence, will lower her gaze. Then one of her friends, who is there for that purpose, can reply positively to the husband's questions, while the girl glances at him shyly, as if confirming the replies.

If the young girl knows the man well, she will drape a garland of flowers around his neck, and he will take the opportunity to caress her breasts with his fingertips. If she tries to stop him, he promises not to do so again, as long as she keeps on embracing him.

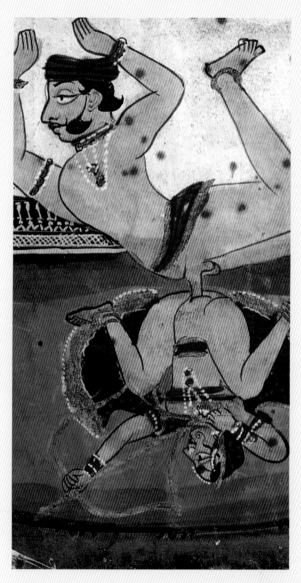

When she hugs him around the neck, he will occasionally stroke the nape of her neck and her back, and will press his hand against her legs and belly as a sign of his desire to make love. If the girl continues to resist, he threatens – in a joking manner – to make nail and teeth marks on her breasts and arms, and similar marks on his own flesh, and then he will tell everyone that she was the one who made the marks on his body!

During the subsequent nights, when the girl begins to surrender to her husband, he must caress her entire body and smother it with kisses, place his hands on her thighs and massage them gently, ascending from there to her groin. If she tries to stop him, he must ask her: "What's wrong with that?" and persuade her to let him do as he pleases.

When he reaches her genitals, he strokes her crotch and her Yoni, loosens her outer belt and the belt of her undergarment, and massages her naked thighs, taking advantage of every opportunity to touch her, but he does not insist on actual intercourse. Only then does he tell her about the sixty-four arts of the *Kama Sutra*, reveal his love to her, and let her know what he expects of her.

He has to promise to be faithful to her, and to declare repeatedly that he will never take another woman in her place.

112

Finally, when he has overcome her shyness, he will initiate sexual intercourse, without fearing resistance from her.

By acting in this way, the man will gain the girl's love and trust.

Love is not achieved by force, against the girl's will. A girl whose body was used for intercourse against her wishes despises the man whose behavior showed that he did not respect her feelings.

Relationships with women who are married to other men

 man is permitted to seduce another man's wife if he is prepared to risk his life for his love. There are ten degrees of love between a man and a married woman, according to the external signs revealed by the man. These are expressed in: glances, distraction, daydreams, sleeplessness, weight loss, eschewing entertainment, eccentric behavior, madness, fainting spells, and death.

A young woman who is overcome with passion reveals this fact in her conduct, conversation, and body movements.

The man's good looks always attract the woman, and the woman's beauty always attracts the man; however, in most cases, there are other circumstances that prevent the attraction from developing into full-blown love.

A woman in love reveals her love, without thinking whether this is good or bad. When the man courts her, she will reject him at first, but afterward she will surrender to his persistent wooing.

The man, on the other hand, does not reveal his love, and controls his emotions by force and logic. Even if he is incapable of thinking of anything but a particular woman, he will reject her advances.

Sometimes, the man will forego further attempts to seduce the woman after he has failed once. When he succeeds in his conquest, he will pretend to be indifferent.

A woman can reject the courting of a man for the following reasons:

Fidelity to her husband; fear of giving birth to a bastard; lack of a suitable opportunity to react favorably; hostility toward the suitor; caste differences; the fear that he loves another woman; uncertainty as to the suitor's place of residence; the fear that he is extremely close to his friends; diffidence due to a high-ranking, clever and handsome man; fear of losing her good reputation; fear of the strength of her desire, if she is a Deer woman; her suitor's bad reputation; his defects and deficiencies. If she is an Elephant woman, she fears that he is a Hare man; or that her husband sent the suitor in order to test her loyalty; fear of revealing her genitals and her sagging flesh; fear of being found out and becoming a laughing-stock.

Men who are loved by women

en who are loved by women have the following characteristics:
They are men who are well-versed in the art of love; men who know how to make time pass pleasantly with stories and deeds; men who have lived with women since childhood; men who know how to gain women's trust; men who give gifts; men who are articulate; men who know how to fulfill women's wishes; men who have not yet had a woman; masseurs; men who acknowledge their own weaknesses; men who are desired by upper-caste women; handsome men; men whom the women have known since childhood; neighbors; men who are able to devote themselves wholeheartedly to sexual intercourse, even if they are slaves; men who are the lovers of female relatives; recently-widowed men; men who love entertainment and do a lot of socializing; generous men; men who are aware of their strength and power – Bull men; men who are courageous and full of initiative; men who are superior to the woman's husband in knowledge, appearance, good qualities, and generosity; men who are well-dressed and live lives of luxury.

A man who is loved by women never attempts to seduce a young girl who is afraid of him, or a girl who does not trust him, or a girl whose virtue is being guarded, or a stepmother.

When a woman fiercely opposes a man's advances, he must desist immediately – but if, even while she is resisting him, she persists in looking upon him favorably and dropping subtle hints of encouragement, he must continue until he gains her love.

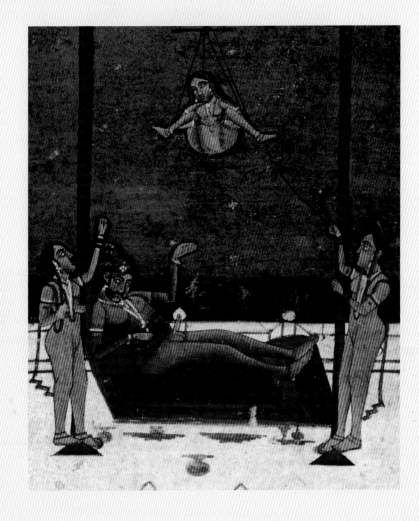

121

Obligations of an older wife toward her husband's younger wives

ven if his wife is still alive, a man is permitted to take other wives, for the following reasons: insanity, or a broken spirit; a feeling of revulsion for her; barrenness; refusal to grant him conjugal rights.

If a woman is barren, it is her duty to persuade her husband to take another wife, and to grant the new wife higher status than her own; she must behave like a sister toward the new wife, advising her, and helping her take care of her children as if they were her own. Her conduct is the same with the new wife's servants and relatives.

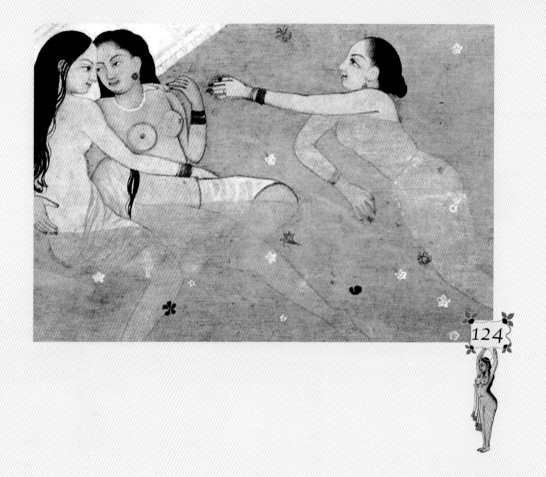

If there are several wives, the eldest among them must make a pact with the one who is second to her in age and status, and the two of them must try to create dissent between the younger wives, as well as unite all the wives against the one who is the husband's favorite. The eldest must always make the favored wife out to be wicked, quarrelsome, and loathed by the other wives.

In any event, the eldest wife must try to separate the husband from his favorite wife, otherwise the latter will quickly usurp her place and status.

Ways of getting rid of an unwanted lover

y mocking and criticizing his leadership; by laughing at his failures in his face, and by stamping on his foot.

By discussing subjects about which he knows nothing, by undermining his self-confidence, and by seeking the company of men who are superior to him in knowledge and education.

By opposing him in everything, and by criticizing men whose shortcomings are similar to his.

By casually dismissing his attempts to arouse sexual desire; by turning her face away when he tries to kiss her mouth, and shifting her body away when he tries to kiss her Jagbana; by protesting about his scratches and bites, and not responding to his caresses; by lying motionless during sexual intercourse.

By demanding copulation when he is worn out and exhausted.

By scoffing at his fidelity.

By not responding when he begins to caress and kiss her.

By going to sleep or leaving the house every time he feels like making love during the day.

By imitating his habits and speech.

By laughing at his actions for no apparent reason – and by not laughing when he is trying to tell jokes and be amusing.

By giving her servants significant looks.

By cutting him off in the middle of a sentence, and changing the subject.

By not paying attention when he is talking.

By discussing his shortcomings with her servants – in his presence.

By pretending not to notice that he is approaching.

By asking him to do things of which he is not capable.

And finally – by dismissing him.

128

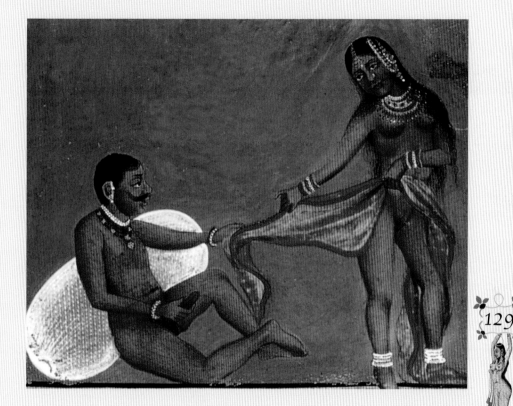

There is a saying which is appropriate not only for courtesans and prostitutes:

"The professional obligation of the courtesan is to enter a relationship after due consideration and finding out if the man can give her what she wants; then she must devote herself to the man with whom she is living, take whatever she can from him, and finally, after milking him dry, dismiss him. A courtesan who lives in this way, like a married woman, becomes rich without tiring herself out with numerous lovers."

129

Courtesans, also called prostitutes

 hen a courtesan loves the man to whom she is giving herself, her actions are natural. When she does it for the money, she is faking it and acting for her own material gain – but she must behave as if she is acting out of love, since men trust women who act as if they are in love with them. While she is showing him her love, she must act as if she does not expect anything in return.

The courtesan should dress well and stand at the doorway to her house – without exposing herself too much – looking out onto the street. She must behave cordially to anyone who can help her find men and become rich, or who can protect her from harm and injury: city guards and policemen, clerks and officers of the courts, fortune tellers, powerful people and lenders, teachers, entertainers, clowns, flower sellers, barbers and beggars, and anyone else who can help advance her ambitions as a courtesan.

Men she may consort with because she will earn money from them are: young, debt-free men, civil servants with a fixed income, rich heirs, male prostitutes who desire to conceal their profession, philanthropists, men of high status, successful businessmen, the only son of a rich father, the king's physicians, and casual acquaintances.

The courtesan can enter a relationship with men who have good qualities – not for money, but rather for love or the desire to raise her status. These men are: poets, storytellers, noblemen, learned men, and men with good qualities; powerful, handsome men, men who are known for their love of sexual intercourse and their expertise in it, but are not totally controlled by women.

The courtesan must be beautiful and pleasant, able to enjoy the sexual act which stems from love, always search for ways to improve her lovemaking and to gain experience in sex. She must always seek variety in the pleasures of sex.

The courtesan who is not well-versed in all sixty-four arts of the *Kama Sutra* will not succeed at what she does.

Money is the prime motivator in the courtesan's life, and she never sacrifices money for love. Only in this way can she achieve the pleasures of the flesh and escape poverty and wretchedness.

133

The king's wives, and his treatment of them

he king's wives lead lives of serenity, wealth and amusements. They are never expected to do hard work, which would exhaust them. They go to theaters, festivals and musical performances. There, they are treated with respect, and are offered food and drink.

They are not permitted to leave the harem unaccompanied. Only female visitors, who have been invited beforehand, may enter the harem.

Every morning, the lady's personal maid brings gifts of flowers, lilies, and garments from her lady to the king. The king offers the gifts and clothes to his wives, just as he distributes the clothes that he wore the previous day.

In the afternoon, the king, in full regalia, visits his wives, who have put on their most magnificent clothes in honor of his visit. He shows them signs of respect and appreciation, and directs them to their places. Then he begins a merry conversation with them.

136

Afterward, he visits the virgins in his harem, the courtesans and the Biadras, each in her own room.

When the king has concluded his afternoon rest, he is approached by the woman whose job it is to announce the name of the woman with whom he will spend the night. She is accompanied by the maids of the woman whose turn it is, and by the maids of women who are ill, or who missed their turn for some reason.

The members of the king's family present the king with gifts and perfumes sent to him by the women – those whose turn it is and those who missed their turn – and the king, by choosing one of the gifts upon which the woman's seal appears, makes his choice known in this way.

Some kings fortify themselves with potions so that they can pleasure several wives each night. Some pleasure only their favorites, and ignore the others. Most kings tend to go in order and give each woman a turn.

Cases in which love is permitted

 hen there is love between a married couple of the same caste and social status, love is permitted and appreciated by everyone.

When a man loves a woman of a higher social status, or a similar-caste woman who is someone else's wife, it is forbidden love.

Love does not relate in any way to women of lower status, to women who are outcastes, to prostitutes or divorcees. With these women, any expressions of desire and all the tricks of sex aim only to achieve pleasure, and not to experience love.

Women with whom sexual intercourse is permitted without fear of sin are known as Niaykas – young women who are not dependent on anyone, courtesans and women who are married for the second time.

Some expand on the above list, adding widows, courtesans' daughters, servants prior to losing their virginity, and even woman of the same caste who reach maturity without getting married.

There are people who justify intercourse with a married woman under certain circumstances, some examples of which follow:

"This woman desires me, and has already had intercourse with many men; although she belongs to a higher caste than I do, she behaves like a courtesan; therefore I can make love with her without it being a sin."

"Her husband is my enemy and can cause me harm; if his wife falls in love with me, she is likely to change his hostility toward me into friendship."

"If I win the love of this woman, it will help me accomplish a certain mission which will be extremely profitable to me."

"I have no fortune or assets, and sexual intercourse with this woman can enrich me."

"This woman knows me well, and is privy to all my secrets, and if I do not make love to her, she can do me harm."

"Her husband dishonored my wife, and now, in revenge, I have to dishonor his."

After the man has overcome the woman's shyness, they must exchange gifts, clothes, rings and flowers. His gifts must be stunning in their beauty and value. He must ask her to put the flowers he gave her in her hair, or to hold them in her hand. Then he must take her and embrace and kiss her. Finally, after they have exchanged betel and flowers, he must caress and touch her Yoni, and when she becomes aroused, he can complete the act of seduction.

When he is pursuing one woman, the man does not attempt to seduce another simultaneously. However, after he succeeds with the first one, and enjoys her charms for a long time, he can give her a valuable gift, and go off in search of the next conquest.

The major part of the man's efforts are aimed at entering the woman's house and conversing with her. He has to reveal his intentions in words, and after he has received her tacit consent, he initiates his strategies for obtaining his heart's desire.

A woman who does not attempt to conceal her love is like a fruit that is ripe for plucking.

"Passion which is aroused naturally, nurtured with art and preserved with devotion, needs strength and security. A clever and considerate man understands the innermost thoughts of the woman and refrains from doing anything that may hurt her or make things difficult for her. This is how he will obtain and keep her love."

A man who has learnt to conquer other men's wives through his skill in the principles of the *Kama Sutra* will never be cuckolded.

The arts of seduction and sexual intercourse are conveyed here for the benefit of everyone – not only so that a man can seduce another man's wife, but also to teach a man how to safeguard his own wife from other men.

After the man gets to know the woman, and if she reveals her love through external signs and body nuances, the man must go all the way; if she is a virgin, he must be careful and considerate.

143